THE PRIMROSE PATH
by
Gillian Plowman

Published by:
New Playwrights' Network
35 Sandringham Road
Macclesfield
Cheshire
SK10 1QB

ISBN 0 86319 174 6

THE PRIMROSE PATH.

It is a composite set which includes Greenhouse, Sitting room and Kitchen. This can be as simple or well-dressed as the Director wishes, but there are certain properties and furniture which are necessary to the play. The open-framed doors may well be dispensed with.

BRIDGET is in the Greenhouse repotting some plants. She is wearing dungarees. JAMES enters the Greenhouse, having come from the bedroom through the sitting room and kitchen and in through the greenhouse door. He walks slowly as though he is not quite sure what he is supposed to be doing.

BRIDGET: Oh!
JAMES: Oh?
BRIDGET: I didn't think you'd be up.
JAMES: It's nine o'clock.

BRIDGET: I thought you'd lie in today. I was going to bring you a cup of tea later.
JAMES: Breakfast in bed?
BRIDGET: If you like.
JAMES: I don't like.
BRIDGET: Sorry.
JAMES: Is that what you took the day off for?
BRIDGET: I took it off to be with you.
JAMES: On my first day...
BRIDGET: Do you want breakfast?
JAMES: No.
BRIDGET: You've got your suit on.
JAMES: You're observant.
BRIDGET: Sorry.
JAMES: For the second time.
BRIDGET: Is there anything in the paper?
JAMES: News, views...
BRIDGET: Any jobs?

He shakes his head, She returns to the plants.

JAMES: What are you doing?
BRIDGET: Repotting the house plants. They like a change. A bigger pot. Gives them a lease of life.
JAMES: Perhaps you could repot me.
BRIDGET: Cheer up, James. Hundreds of people get made redundant.
JAMES: I never thought I'd be one of them. What will you do, Bridget?
BRIDGET: Anything you like, eh?
JAMES: Mmmm.
BRIDGET: I should go and get changed. Put your jeans on.
JAMES: And then what?
BRIDGET: Anything you like. *(Pause)*
JAMES: I've thought of something.
BRIDGET: What?
JAMES: I'm going back to bed. Coming?
BRIDGET: At nine o'clock on a Monday morning?
JAMES: One of the perks of having no job to go to.
BRIDGET: But I have...

JAMES: Yes, I know you have. But if you've taken a day off to be with me, come and spend it with me.

They return to the bedroom through the kitchen and sitting room. On the way through the kitchen JAMES switches on the electric kettle.

We'll have coffee...after.

BRIDGET takes off her shoes in the kitchen before going into the sitting room. She glances at her watch before going into the bedroom. JAMES follows her. PRIMROSE enters downstage. She is a tramp. Who can tell what age. Shapeless coat, worn shoes etc. She wears a rucksack. She checks that no-one is about, and enters the greenhouse. She finishes off Bridget's cup of tea that has been left there.

PRIMROSE: Nice cup o' tea. Could sink another of them.
　　　　　Now then. Off with your coat.
　　　　　Thank you, Irene.
　　　　　Where's the soap? Got the soap...Ah, yes. Smells nice.
(She has a wash in the watering can, using a tiny piece of soap that she has in a little tin. She combs her hair carefully, talking to herself all the time) Nice shower. Ought to get a bit of shampoo, Irene. Could do with getting to the shops. Lovely hair you got, Primrose. Nice when it's done nice. Not like yours, Tatty head you got, Irene. Bet it itches a bit an' all.

She gives herself a good scratch and lays down on the lounger, falling into a fitful, snoring sleep. JAMES enters the sitting room in his dressing gown. BRIDGET follows.

BRIDGET: It doesn't matter.
JAMES: Of course it does.
BRIDGET: It doesn't. I'll make some coffee.
JAMES: I'll make it. I might as well do something useful.

THE PRIMROSE PATH

BRIDGET: Oh, James. Stop feeling so sorry for yourself.
JAMES: It's you I feel sorry for.
BRIDGET: I don't mind.
JAMES: You can get back to your greenhouse!
BRIDGET: That's unfair.
JAMES: *I* mind. Don't you see? *I* mind!
BRIDGET: It's probably because it's Monday morning...or something.

He goes into the kitchen, she back to the bedroom. PRIMROSE snores herself awake.

PRIMROSE: Sunday, Monday, Tuesday, Wednesday...I wonder what day it is? No church bells. Not Sunday. Good. Mr and Mrs at work. *(She sits up)* Saturday! Bulldozers! *(She counts on her fingers)* Wednesday. Thursday, Friday, Saturday. Three days! Where have you been? The frogs, yes. Went to the reservoir. Been to Irene's. Lovely house - Irene's. Likes to see me. Makes me welcome as the Queen.

During the above, JAMES has been making coffee. BRIDGET enters the kitchen, dressed.

BRIDGET: Let's pretend it's a Bank Holiday Monday. A long weekend. Like all those Mondays we have off in May.
JAMES: Bridget - there's a terrible tightness across my chest. It's real, and I'm frightened to death.
BRIDGET: Oh, James. *(She holds him)*
JAMES: How would you feel, if it was the other way round? Tell me the truth, Bridget. What would you do?
BRIDGET: A woman can always find something to do.
JAMES: What?
BRIDGET: Write a novel. Have a baby...
JAMES: You can't have a baby.
BRIDGET: So, I did something else. That's what you have to do.
JAMES: Write a novel...?
BRIDGET: Why not?
JAMES: I don't know about anything.
BRIDGET: Make it up. It's fiction.
JAMES: I haven't got much imagination.

THE PRIMROSE PATH

BRIDGET: Don't write a novel then. Do something else. Set up in business. Make spinning wheels.

JAMES: That's not much of a business.

BRIDGET: Invent a new way of connecting an electric plug. An idiot-proof method - for idiots like me. Make it, market it - that's your forte.

JAMES: That needs capital.

BRIDGET: You've got capital...gold-plated handshake.

JAMES: It's a risk.

BRIDGET: So was marrying me.

JAMES: That was a necessity. I had no choice. I couldn't live without you.

BRIDGET: With someone else you could have had children.

JAMES: Thank God we haven't, as it's turned out. Can't support them.

BRIDGET: I could. I can support you. You invest your gold-plated handshake and take the risk. I can make enough for us to live on in the meantime.

JAMES: It wouldn't be enough anyway.

BRIDGET: The grass needs cutting.

JAMES: What?

BRIDGET: It needs cutting. You might as well cut it. I'll lounge in a deck chair and watch you working. It is my day off after all.

JAMES: So I'm reduced to chores now, am I?

BRIDGET: We could have the best-kept garden round these parts.

JAMES: Great.

BRIDGET: Then you could wash the cars. I'll turn my deck chair round.

JAMES: We'll have to sell one.

BRIDGET: Why not? We'll only need one.

JAMES: For you to go to work in?

BRIDGET: No, I can get a bus. For you. You can use it.

JAMES: What for? The shopping?

BRIDGET: For whatever you like.

JAMES: *I don't know what I like!*

BRIDGET: You did before. Never enough time to do the interesting things in, you said.

JAMES: What were they?

BRIDGET: Football, fishing, films, photography - what else

    begins with 'f'?

JAMES: Finding a job.

BRIDGET: Something will turn up.

JAMES: Probably the same day you get pregnant. *(Pause)*

BRIDGET: That was cruel.

JAMES: I know. Shout at me. Tell me off.

BRIDGET: Is that what you want?

JAMES: All this understanding wife bit. - it doesn't help.

BRIDGET: I should have gone to work today, let you get on with it.

JAMES: Hullo, dear, had a good day? What have I been doing? Oh, I've been busy. Put the washing out, then, damn me, it rained, so I got it in again although it wasn't dry which was a nuisance.

BRIDGET: We've got a tumble dryer, so you don't have to put it out at all...

JAMES: But it's so much nicer, don't you think, with the fresh air, wind and sun blowing through it.

BRIDGET: Stop it! Stop it, James. It's not your fault - you weren't incompetent or anything - it's just the times we live in. There's nothing so remarkable about us. We're just 'now' people. You're out of work. I'm in work. Six months time it could be the other way round. Luck of the draw. Doesn't mean anything, we just have to get on with whatever needs doing in order to live. Get by, if you like. But there's nothing wrong with having a go at living.

JAMES: Coffee.

BRIDGET: Thanks.

The phone rings. BRIDGET answers it.

PRIMROSE: Hullo, Primrose...Had a nice holiday? Yes thank you, Irene. Come and sit by the fire. I'll make you a nice cup of tea. Irene, you don't happen to have a little drop of sherry, do you? Of course, of course, saving it just for you. Best sherry. Cream sherry. Knew it was your favourite. Oh, Irene, you do like me to come and visit you, don't you? Yes, I do. Do you know, Primrose, you're my oldest friend. I'd never do anything to hurt you.

'Cept you took my husband away from me.
Primrose, I didn't do that. How could you say such a thing? He wanted to come. And look at the trouble it saves you. You don't have to cook and clean for him any more now, do you? You can be free to do whatever you want to do now. And you're always welcome to come to our house any time you like. I'll always have a bottle of the best cream sherry waiting for you...you'll be as welcome as the Queen.

BRIDGET: That was the office. Madeleine's got the 'flu - I'll have to go in.

JAMES: Fortunate for you.

BRIDGET: Why?

JAMES: You won't have to put up with me all day.

BRIDGET: Perhaps you'll have snapped out of it by tonight. You could give it a try.

JAMES: I could, yes, I could. If I try very hard, I could. I could be a different man by the time you get back tonight.

BRIDGET: If you're doing the washing up, I've left my coffee mug in the greenhouse.

JAMES: Why don't you leave me a list.

BRIDGET: Use your initiative.

JAMES: Do what I like ...

BRIDGET: Oh, James. Do what the hell you like!

Exit BRIDGET into the bedroom.
PRIMROSE sits up and warms her hands in front of the heater.

PRIMROSE: I can't afford to live on my own, you know, Irene. I'll have to get my husband back ... Have another sherry, Primrose ... Thanks, I don't mind if I do ... We don't either of us need a man. They're an encumberance. Awful nuisance. But one of us has got to look after this one, and you'll be better off without. He tells you off, doesn't he? When you drink too much sherry ... It's not the sherry, Irene. It's his whisky. Tells me off for drinking that ... Well, there you are then, but why is it his whisky? ... Because he buys it ...

I buy it, Irene. I do all the shopping ... Well, he pays
for it ... He pays for the cheese as well, and the bread,
but he doesn't lay claim to them. Yet the whisky is his.
Like the shaving cream is his ... Well, there you are
then, Primrose. You're better off without him, then the
whisky's yours ... She's a stupid bitch is Irene. Now I
can't afford any whisky!

*She lays down on the lounger again and JAMES enters the
greenhouse in his dressing gown. They stare at each
other. He pulls the dressing gown around him.*

PRIMROSE: Bulldozers!
JAMES: Pardon?
PRIMROSE: It's all right. I've seen it all before. Men's bits.
JAMES: Who the hell are you?
PRIMROSE: Could you pass me coat, dear ... I took it off
because it's warm in here.
JAMES: It's a greenhouse.
PRIMROSE: Got a nice little heater.
JAMES: What are you doing here?
PRIMROSE: My mistake. I thought it was a weekday. Should have
checked the cars. No church bells, though. Must be
Saturday, eh?
JAMES: It's Monday.
PRIMROSE: You ill, then? Shouldn't be out of the 'ouse in that
shortie thing. Catch yer death.
JAMES: I'm not ill.
PRIMROSE: Not staying home for the holidays? Oh, dear me.
JAMES: Would you mind removing yourself from my greenhouse.
PRIMROSE: Yes, I'm only passing through.
JAMES: Oh are you?
PRIMROSE: I don't smell. I wash meself regular. I got soap,
see. You have a sniff. *(She raises her arm)* See, I don't
smell do I? You smell nice.
JAMES: Thank you. I mean ...
PRIMROSE: A gent aren't you. Nice manners, can't help
yourself. You're like Irene. She's got nice manners, on
the surface, but deep down inside ... tut, tut.
JAMES: Look ...

THE PRIMROSE PATH

PRIMROSE: Now you...wouldn't hurt a fly, you. Would yer. I bet people put upon you, don't they? Always doing someone a favour, I bet. Well, here's one who won't be putting on you. Primrose Cornwallis at your service. How do you do?

He takes her proffered hand and shakes it before realising what he is doing.

JAMES: Would you mind going ...

PRIMROSE: I'll give it to yer straight. I am itinerant. Got no home. Just keep moving. Not my fault, just the way it is. And I wondered if by any chance you might have a bit of hot water and a tea bag, to see me on my way ...

JAMES: I don't think I ought to ...

PRIMROSE: Your wife in?

JAMES: No. She's gone to work.

PRIMROSE: Nice woman, your wife. Pretty. All about. Got a good job, has she?

JAMES: She's a secretary.

PRIMROSE: Oh, that's good. Clever. You know, newspaper's a marvellous thing for lining shoes. Don't half keep yer feet warm. If I could just have me cup of tea, I could cut up yer yesterday's paper for new linings. If you've got some scissors.

JAMES: I don't know where the scissors are.

PRIMROSE: Ere. You 'aven't got the sack, have you?

JAMES: And you can't have a cup of tea.

PRIMROSE: There you are, you see. Put me finger on it, haven't I? No point in taking it out on me. Not my fault you got the sack is it. And you a gentleman and all. Remember what Baden-Powell said. 'The sign of a gentleman is not how other people treat you, but how you treat other people.' He's right, isn't he? Think how you'd feel without your morning cup of tea.

JAMES: I prefer coffee myself.

PRIMROSE: Well, there you are then. I'll have a coffee with you. Keep you company. I won't bother to lace me shoes up now then. Wait till we've found the scissors. Have you tried all the drawers in the kitchen? No, you ain't tried none of them, have you? Typical man. *(She pulls her shoes* *on)* Right, lead the way. *(They go into the kitchen)* It's a posh name, isn't it? Primrose Cornwallis. Don't suit me really. It *was* Jenkins. Cornwallis is me married name. Kept it on. *(She starts opening the kitchen drawers)*

JAMES: I'll do that.

PRIMROSE: Where's your old papers, then?

JAMES: I'll get them.

PRIMROSE: Oh, that's nice.

JAMES: What?

PRIMROSE: Nearly as posh as mine.

JAMES: Eh?

PRIMROSE: Your name. On this envelope. James P.J. Kellaway. What's the P.J. stand for? *(She has picked up a letter. Which he takes off her)*

JAMES: So you can read?

PRIMROSE: I am both literate and numerate...

JAMES: And itinerate! *(She is poking about)* Look, sit down. Here. That's right. And don't move and don't touch anything. *(He gets the things)* Papers. Scissors.

PRIMROSE: Where were they?

JAMES: In the kitchen drawer.

PRIMROSE: Told yer.

JAMES: And here's your coffee.

PRIMROSE: Thank you very much, James. Aren't you having one?

JAMES: Not just now.

PRIMROSE: You couldn't spare a bit of bread, could you? *(He gets a plate, plonks a slice of bread on it and puts it in front of her)* Is that how you'd eat it? *(He puts the slice of bread into the toaster)* Pity to put just one bit in. *(He puts another slice in and gets butter and marmalade out)* Aren't you going to get dressed?

JAMES: After you've gone.

PRIMROSE: Ain't heard that in years. Not from a man. I'll get dressed after you've gone. *(She turns serious)* I'm not a thief you know. I won't take nothing. I don't need anything other than what you're giving me. Breakfast. I won't hurt nothing. You can leave me here quite safe. You got to trust people in this world, Jimmy.

JAMES: Help yourself to the toast when it pops up.

Exit JAMES. PRIMROSE gets the toast, butters it and puts marmalade on. She also sticks her fingers into the pot and licks them. She finds a packet of biscuits in a cupboard and pockets them. She finds a tea towel and puts it over her lap as a serviette as she sits down to eat. She talks all the time.

PRIMROSE: You see, Irene - I've got friends all over. Nice people, all of them. If it wasn't for you, Irene, looking after himself for me, I wouldn't have got out and about, meeting all these people. Now here's a nice man, who's got the sack. Eh? Not very nice, that, is it? I know. I got the sack once. From being a wife. So he needs a friend. And what better than one who understands. See, Irene? You cow... *(JAMES returns dressed in sweater and jeans)* That's better.

JAMES: Don't make yourself at home.

PRIMROSE: Thank you very much. I will. Tell me all about it then. You getting the sack.

JAMES: I was made redundant.

PRIMROSE: What's the difference.

JAMES: Means it wasn't my fault.

PRIMROSE: It was really.

JAMES: How?

PRIMROSE: For choosing the wrong line of business in the first place.

JAMES: You wouldn't understand.

PRIMROSE: Oh I understand all right. I did it meself. Made the wrong choice. Nice toast.

JAMES: Thank you.

PRIMROSE: Wrong husband.

JAMES: What happened to him?

PRIMROSE: He bogged off. Couldn't keep me home on, so I became itinerant.

JAMES: You mean you're a tramp?

PRIMROSE: Yes.

JAMES: Sleeping in people's greenhouses.

PRIMROSE: Yeh.

JAMES: Cadging coffee and toast.

PRIMROSE: You offered.

THE PRIMROSE PATH

JAMES: Not that I remember.
PRIMROSE: Tell you what - I'll make you a cup.
JAMES: All right.
PRIMROSE: And meself another.
JAMES: Think I'm a right rip-off, don't you? I bet you turn up here every bloody day from now on.
PRIMROSE: Not without an invitation I don't.
JAMES: How long have you been sleeping in our greenhouse? *(She gives him the coffee)* Thanks.
PRIMROSE: Only about ten minutes.
JAMES: I didn't mean that...
PRIMROSE: I didn't have a very good night last night. Reckon there must have been a witch hunt or something going on. Police and folks all over, all night. Couldn't get a wink.
JAMES: They didn't get you then.
PRIMROSE: What for? I don't break no laws.
JAMES: Trespassing for one.
PRIMROSE: No, that's not a criminal offence.
JAMES: Breaking and entering is.
PRIMROSE: Only with intent; and my only intent was to sleep. What day did you say it was?
JAMES: Monday.
PRIMROSE: I thought it was. Thought I couldn't be wrong. Not very often I'm wrong, although Friday seemed likely.
JAMES: Where do you sleep? Apart from my greenhouse.
PRIMROSE: I often walk through the night, you know. It's a fine thing. Moonlight and owls, little rabbits, all sorts. The world's mine at night. Always liked the night-life, me. Got any music. *(She switches on the radio which happens to be playing some up-tempo music)* Back in the days before I was a virgin - you wouldn't believe it - but I had a nice figure. Used to dance the night away. Music, cigarettes, drop of booze. You haven't got a cigarette, have yer?
JAMES: There you are, you see. You're cadging.
PRIMROSE: Well, offer then.
JAMES: We don't smoke.
PRIMROSE: Not fashionable, is it? What about a drink? I'd love a glass of sherry.

THE PRIMROSE PATH

JAMES: Well, you're not getting one, not at this time on a Monday morning.

PRIMROSE: When?

JAMES: Not ever. Come on, now, on your way.

PRIMROSE: The thing is, it doesn't matter. If you're itinerant like me, or redundant like you, it doesn't matter if it's Monday morning. Morning's the same as evening. Monday's the same as Friday, thirty's the same as fifty, man's the same as woman. You and me, we could be anybody, anywhere, anytime, enjoying a glass of sherry.

JAMES: Bridget, my wife, said to me this morning - you can do anything you like today.

PRIMROSE: Bet she didn't mean it though.

JAMES: What?

PRIMROSE: All right for her to talk. But she's a wife, and sure as eggs have shells, she'll only mean the things that she approves of. She wouldn't approve of this, would she?

JAMES: What?

PRIMROSE: You giving me sherry in the kitchen.

JAMES: No, she'd say the sitting room's the place to have sherry.

PRIMROSE: Right, off we go then. Sitting room. Which way? This way?

JAMES: No! I mean yes, that's the way, but you're not going in there.

She has gone into the sitting room.

PRIMROSE: Oh, it's nice. Nicer than Irene's. It's nicer than your place, Irene. It's sort of velvet and pink. Tasteful. You never did have no taste, Irene, and that wart you live with don't know his backside from his elbow when it comes to quality living. *(She sees a decanter on the sideboard)* Is that it? The sherry? You don't want to leave it out, dear.

JAMES: You're not having sherry. You're not having anything. Put that down and get out. I've had enough of you, thank you very much.

PRIMROSE: It's a lovely bottle.

JAMES: Decanter.

PRIMROSE: Does it come in that?

JAMES: It comes in a bottle.

PRIMROSE: Then you put it in here?

JAMES: Yes.

PRIMROSE: Look at that, Irene.

JAMES: Put it down.

PRIMROSE: I won't drop it.

JAMES: Give it to me. *(She hands it to him. He takes it. She immediately holds out a glass)* On your bike, Primrose.

PRIMROSE: Oh, you are funny, you are. On your bike. I'd like a bike. You got a bike? Come on, pour it out. You can do whatever you like.

JAMES: What I like is not pouring it out.

PRIMROSE: What I like is not spitting in your face.

JAMES: What?

PRIMROSE: What I like is not pouring this all over the carpet. *(She grabs the decanter off him and runs away)* You should see the carpet, Irene - it's white. Shows every stain.

JAMES: Be careful!

PRIMROSE: You be careful or I'll miss the glass. *(He approaches slowly and she pours slowly. She gives him the glass)* That's for you.

JAMES: I don't want one.

PRIMROSE: You bloody drink it or I'll tip this all out. All of it. *(As he hesitates, she starts to pour and he has a sip)* All of it. *(He drinks it all)* Now another.

JAMES: This is stupid. It's you who wanted the drink.

PRIMROSE: I'm not going to drink it out of the bottle, am I? What do you think I am? *(He gets another glass and holds it out)* Both of them. *(He holds them both out. She pours sherry into them both. She raises her glass to him, and he reluctantly touches it with his)* Cheers.

JAMES: Cheers.

PRIMROSE: Nice, innit? Shall we sit down?

JAMES: No, we shall not sit down. *(She sits down)*

PRIMROSE: Would you go and fetch the scissors and newspaper.

JAMES: No.

PRIMROSE: Finish your drink first. *(She starts to tip the*

THE PRIMROSE PATH

*decanter **again** and he finishes his drink)* Off you go
then. *(He **gets** the scissors and paper from the kitchen.
She gives him another glass of sherry)*

JAMES: I don't like you, you know.

PRIMROSE: Neither does Irene, but she pretends she does. Not
like you. You come straight out with it. You're honest.

JAMES: Yes, I am honest. And I don't like you.

PRIMROSE: It's not me you don't like. It's your wife, and this
carpet.

JAMES: I love my wife. And this carpet.

PRIMROSE: If you didn't have a wife, and a carpet, it wouldn't
matter who poured sherry over it. Because it wouldn't
stain on a carpet if you didn't have one, and your wife
wouldn't be cross if you didn't have one.

JAMES: And I wouldn't have any sherry to pour over the carpet.

PRIMROSE: Why not?

JAMES: Because sherry, wives and white carpets go together.
And that's what I've got.

PRIMROSE: That's what you had. Before you were made redundant.

JAMES: Oh yes. Oh shit. I haven't got a job. Primrose, what am
I going to do?

PRIMROSE: Dance!

JAMES: Dance?

PRIMROSE: I'll go and get your wireless. *(She goes into the
kitchen)*

JAMES: Wireless! Ha! Wireless...
*(He picks up the decanter which she has left, and hugs it
to him. She returns and increases the volume on the
radio. He shouts)*
I've put an end to your blackmail. Ha! See? I've got the
dec...sherry bottle.
*(She puts the radio down, picks up the scissors, goes
over to him and cuts off a bit of his hair.)*
Wha...what are you doing? That's my hair.

PRIMROSE: This bit's mine.

JAMES: What d'you do that for?

PRIMROSE: Souvenir.

JAMES: I want it back.

PRIMROSE: Oh no, you can't have it back. In case you're a
naughty boy. If I've got a bit of your hair, I can put a

16

spell on you - whenever you're a naughty boy.

JAMES: You can't do that.

PRIMROSE: I can.

JAMES: You're a witch! Those policemen last night were out hunting you after all.

PRIMROSE: No. They don't know I'm a witch.

JAMES: I want it back.

(He puts the decanter down and lunges after her. He then decides to go back to the bottle in case she gets it and picks it up, drinking every drop out of it)

There. There, you see. Now what are you going to do?

PRIMROSE: That's naughty. That's really naughty. You've drunk it all and it was to share. *(She advances with the scissors)* I'm going to cut your nose off.

JAMES: Nose off...

He makes a fist round his nose and collapses onto the sofa. She proceeds to cut holes in his clothes whilst he watches helplessly.

PRIMROSE: It's not manners that maketh man, but clotheses and noses. If your clothes are cut up and your nose cut off, then what sort of a man are you? I asked Irene that once, 'cos she likes men. She'd like you. She'd take you if she could. Mind, she wouldn't like you in this mess.

JAMES: I hate Irene.

PRIMROSE: You're hating a lot of people today, aren't you?

JAMES: I hate the carpet.

PRIMROSE: You've been a slave to that carpet.

JAMES: And my boss - I've been a slave to him. *(He is still holding his nose)*

PRIMROSE: He's used up a lot of your time. *(She is still cutting holes in his clothes)*

JAMES: And my wife. All she wants is for me to have lots and lots of problems so that she can understand me.

PRIMROSE: Don't have any more then.

JAMES: You haven't, have you?

PRIMROSE: Irene! Have I got problems? No...she took 'em all off me, Irene did. Took me house, me husband, me clothes...being itinerant, you got no problems.

JAMES: Right. I'm off to be itinerant.

PRIMROSE helps him up and he staggers through the kitchen into the greenhouse, and falls onto the lounger. PRIMROSE goes into the bedroom.

Mr Baldwin, you may have come to a momentous decision about who you wish to keep and why you wish to keep them, and I would like to say to you that, despite what I said to you the other week - day - weekday - oh yes, you used up all my Mondays, Tuesdays, Wednesdays and all the others...you used them up and not to mention when I gave you my Saturdays too. And all for what? So you could discard all my days? Well, you can't discard all my days because they are all *my* days, old baldy Baldwin, and from now on, despite what I said about wanting to stay and couldn't somebody else go, beaky baldy Baldwin, you can stuff it. All of it. You can use up as many days as you like, but not mine, because, bandy, beaky, baldy Baldwin - I am going to use them all up myself. And now - Goodnight.

Lights dim to show passing of time. PRIMROSE comes out of the bedroom having found some of BRIDGET's clothes to wear. She finds some more sherry in the sideboard and pours some into her glass. She then pours it back again and pours the whole bottle of sherry into the decanter and then pours some sherry from the decanter into her glass. She sits down.
BRIDGET enters the kitchen.

BRIDGET: Hullo, I'm back. *(PRIMROSE doesn't budge. BRIDGET fills the kettle)* You haven't washed up, lazybones. Hmm. Gone out and left the door unlocked. Oh well ... *(She enters the sitting room)*
PRIMROSE: Hullo, Irene.
BRIDGET: Hullo.
PRIMROSE: Had a busy day?
BRIDGET: I'm sorry?
PRIMROSE: I'll make you a cup of tea, shall I?
BRIDGET: I'm sorry ... you are?

18

THE PRIMROSE PATH

PRIMROSE: It's me, Primrose. Silly thing.

BRIDGET: Is ... my husband about?

PRIMROSE: He's gone for a little lie down.

BRIDGET: Oh.

PRIMROSE: He's had a busy day.

BRIDGET: What's he been doing?

PRIMROSE: Keeping me company, most of the time. But I'm very demanding, you know - I think I've worn him out.

BRIDGET: Are you a friend of his?

PRIMROSE: Oh, yes ...

BRIDGET: I've got a jumper like that. And a skirt ... are you wearing my clothes?

PRIMROSE: You told me to help myself, Irene. Just let yourself in and help yourself to anything you want. So I helped myself to a glass of sherry, some clothes, and your husband's company.

BRIDGET: My name's not Irene. *(PRIMROSE has been making the tea. She puts six spoonfulls in the pot)* You don't need that much.

PRIMROSE: I like a good strong brew.

BRIDGET: I don't.

PRIMROSE: You're not making it, Irene. I am.

BRIDGET: Bridget.

PRIMROSE: Primrose.

BRIDGET: My name's Bridget.

PRIMROSE: Prim by name, rose by nature.

BRIDGET turns on her heel and storms off to the bedroom.

BRIDGET: James! JAMES! *(She goes into the bedroom and comes out again. She goes back to the kitchen)* Where is he?

PRIMROSE: Here's your tea.

BRIDGET: My husband. Where is he?

PRIMROSE: In the greenhouse.

BRIDGET looks at her in amazement and goes to the greenhouse.

BRIDGET: James! Good God, James! What the hell have you done to yourself? Are you all right?

THE PRIMROSE PATH

JAMES: Uhh? Uhh?
BRIDGET: Ugh. You've been drinking. Look at your clothes. What
    have you been doing?
JAMES: Not sure ...

PRIMROSE enters the greenhouse.

PRIMROSE: I don't think Irene approves, James.
BRIDGET: Why are your clothes all cut up?
PRIMROSE: He's a mess, isn't he?
JAMES: Christ, I feel ill.
PRIMROSE: I'm not surprised. He drank a whole thing of sherry.
BRIDGET: What's happened?
JAMES: I can't remember, Irene.
BRIDGET: I'm your wife, Bridget. James, pull yourself
    together, listen to me ...

*He flops and she slaps his face soundly. He curls up in a
foetal position away from her.*

PRIMROSE: He's a little devil, isn't he?
BRIDGET: Where have you come from?
PRIMROSE: I'm a liberated woman, Irene. I come from and go to
    wherever I like. I can do whatever I like.
BRIDGET: Will you please stop calling me Irene! *(PRIMROSE
    picks up a potted plant and deliberately drops it)* Stop
    it!
PRIMROSE: It's over. I've done it. Nothing to stop.
BRIDGET: Stop...Stop being here. Go away. *(PRIMROSE raises
    another plant)* No, don't!
PRIMROSE: Say please, Irene. There's a good girl.
JAMES: Say please, Irene.

BRIDGET pulls JAMES round.
BRIDGET: James, turn round. Look at me. Come on, turn round.
    Look at me and tell me who I am. Why are you holding your
    nose. What's the matter with it?
JAMES: She's going to cut it off.
PRIMROSE: You haven't said please yet.
BRIDGET: Oh shut up. Put that plant down and go away. *(She*

pulls JAMES' hand away from his nose) There's nothing the matter with it. Now, for goodness sake, pull yourself together and get up ...

PRIMROSE drops the second plant which makes BRIDGET jump and JAMES yell and turn back into his foetal position.

BRIDGET: You're insane. I'll have the police on you.
JAMES: She's got my hair.
BRIDGET: What?
JAMES: She's a witch.
BRIDGET: There aren't any witches.
JAMES: Ask her about my hair then.
PRIMROSE: I tell you what. I'll give it you back. I don't need it no more. It's your hair. You have it. You be your own boss from now on. Or shall I give it to Irene?
JAMES: NO! I want it. It's mine. She's got white carpets and sherry decanters. She's not having my hair as well.
PRIMROSE: 'ere you are then.

She holds out her hand. JAMES gets up slowly and takes his hand away from his nose. He takes the hair with relief and visibly regains control of himself.

PRIMROSE: Right, I'm off. Got supper to cook. What's in the fridge, Irene?
BRIDGET: Don't you go near my fridge! *(PRIMROSE picks up another plant and looks at BRIDGET)* I'm going to call the police.
PRIMROSE: It's all right, I'm going now. Nice to have met you both. *(She gives the plant to JAMES)*
BRIDGET: What about my skirt and jumper?
PRIMROSE: I'll keep them, shall I?
BRIDGET: I wouldn't wear them again, not now.
PRIMROSE: Thank you very much, Irene. You always were generous. I'll say that for you. You'll be all right in here, then will you?
BRIDGET: What? Yes...
PRIMROSE: It's got a nice little heater. You'll keep warm.
BRIDGET: What?

PRIMROSE: Right. Goodbye. Look after the wart. Rather you than me, Irene, eh? At least we've agreed on that.

PRIMROSE goes into the house and shuts the kitchen door. She busies herself. JAMES drops the pot.

JAMES: You said I could do anything I liked.
BRIDGET: Within reason. Look at you.
JAMES: So you didn't mean it?
BRIDGET: Yes, I did, but this is ridiculous.
JAMES: In your opinion.
BRIDGET: And not in yours? You *like* being in this mess?
JAMES: You're the only person I ever met in my life, who does exactly what she wants. It's people, possessions, jobs, commitments, manners, behaviour, what your boss thinks, what your wife thinks, what the whole world thinks...all stops you being and doing...what you like. So I'm going now. *(He puts on PRIMROSE's old coat)*
BRIDGET: Where?
JAMES: To walk through the night. With the owls and the rabbits.
BRIDGET: You'll feel better tomorrow.
JAMES: Definitely I will. Goodbye.
BRIDGET: I don't believe this. You're out of your mind.
JAMES: Maybe...you are. Goodbye.
BRIDGET: When will you be back?
JAMES: I don't know. Best to leave the greenhouse unlocked.
BRIDGET: What about me? You can't live without me, you said.

He comes up to her and holds her head in his hands. She relaxes against him. He cuts off a piece of her hair with the garden scissors.

BRIDGET: James! No! No!
JAMES: To take with me. Part of you.

He smiles at her and goes out. BRIDGET holds her head in dismay. She picks up the pots, and straightens the lounger. She goes to the kitchen door and knocks. PRIMROSE is humming as she works.

PRIMROSE: Yes, who is it?
BRIDGET: It's me, Irene. Could I have a cup of tea please.
   (PRIMROSE smiles)

CURTAIN